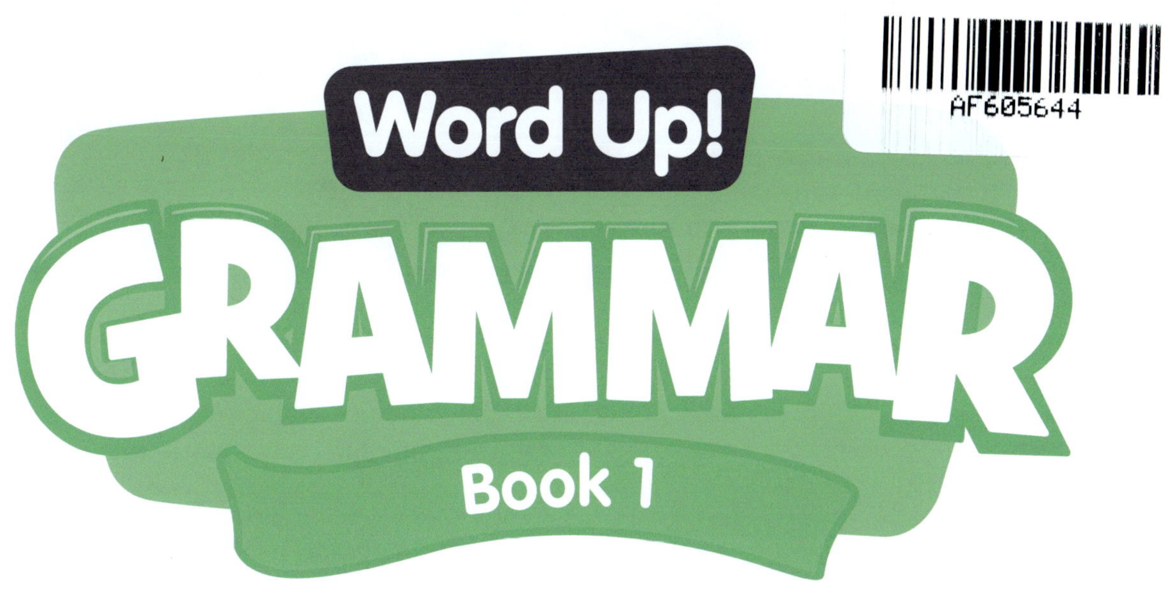

Kerry Shanahan

Why Do We Need Word Up! ?

Word Up! Grammar has been designed in response to an identified classroom need – the need for a differentiated student activity book series linked to the national curriculum. Each unit makes explicit links to the Australian Curriculum content descriptions, general capabilities and cross-curriculum priorities.

Grammar knowledge is best expanded when integrated with other areas of language. **Word Up!** promotes listening, speaking, reading and writing through a diverse range of open and closed activities. The series builds on grammar skills sequentially. Each skill is introduced through varied and engaging texts that stimulate critical and imaginative thinking.

What's in it for teachers?

Word Up! Grammar is a flexible and dynamic student activity series anchored by a sound learning scope and sequence. The book demonstrates how grammar features and structures work at a word, sentence and text level. Grammar is practised and assessed through multimodal, traditional and everyday text.

Each book contains 25 four-page units of work. We recommend integrating one unit per week with your current literacy program. Each unit introduces one or two grammar skills in simple language supported by examples.

What's in it for students?

Topics are broad and level-specific. The series engages students by showing them how grammar lives and breathes in their world.

Through the series, students discover figurative speech through colourful lyric poetry, build expressive noun groups in the lost world of folktales and learn the art of persuasion through modal verbs and emotive language.

Series overview

Word Up! Lower (books 1 and 2) has a special focus on visual literacy for younger learners.

Word Up! Middle and Upper (books 3–6) include annotated sample texts that point out the structure of each text type and, where relevant, point to its language features.

Each book also contains a Scope and Sequence map and a Glossary.

Because we're all different ...

Each **Word Up! Grammar** unit defines the skill, provides examples, models answers and paces activities. Key grammar skills are revised and built on from unit to unit. All students access learning through gradually increasing levels of difficulty. The level of support decreases as students progress through learning and practice.

Differentiated student learning is indicated by three icons:

 indicates basic, closed activities with a high level of student support

 indicates moderate level of student support with a mix of closed and open activity types

 indicates student-led activities that are writing-centred and open-response.

Students can follow the **Word Up!** buzzy bees through each unit. When students have completed all units, they receive a 'Certificate of Completion' at the end of the book.

What's in a Unit?

Unit anchor
Defines the "skill in focus" and provides examples

Text type sample
Short texts provide a learning context

Unit icons
Indicate the question type and level of difficulty

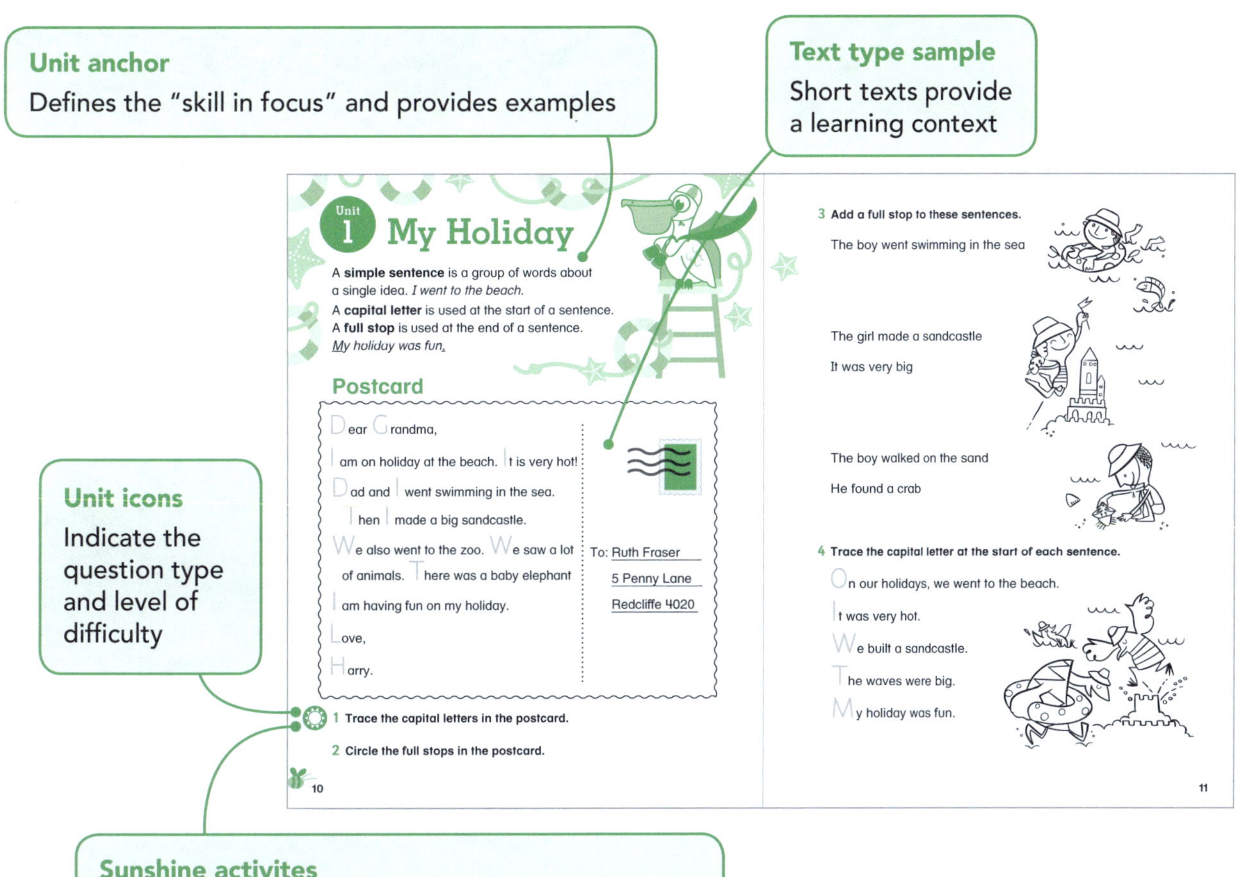

Unit 1

My Holiday

A **simple sentence** is a group of words about a single idea. *I went to the beach.*
A **capital letter** is used at the start of a sentence.
A **full stop** is used at the end of a sentence.
My holiday was fun.

Postcard

Dear Grandma,
I am on holiday at the beach. It is very hot!
Dad and I went swimming in the sea.
Then I made a big sandcastle.
We also went to the zoo. We saw a lot of animals. There was a baby elephant.
I am having fun on my holiday.
Love,
Harry.

To: Ruth Fraser
5 Penny Lane
Redcliffe 4020

1 Trace the capital letters in the postcard.

2 Circle the full stops in the postcard.

10

3 Add a full stop to these sentences.

The boy went swimming in the sea

The girl made a sandcastle
It was very big

The boy walked on the sand
He found a crab

4 Trace the capital letter at the start of each sentence.

On our holidays, we went to the beach.
It was very hot.
We built a sandcastle.
The waves were big.
My holiday was fun.

11

Sunshine activites
Basic, closed questions with extra student support

Moon activities
Closed and open questions

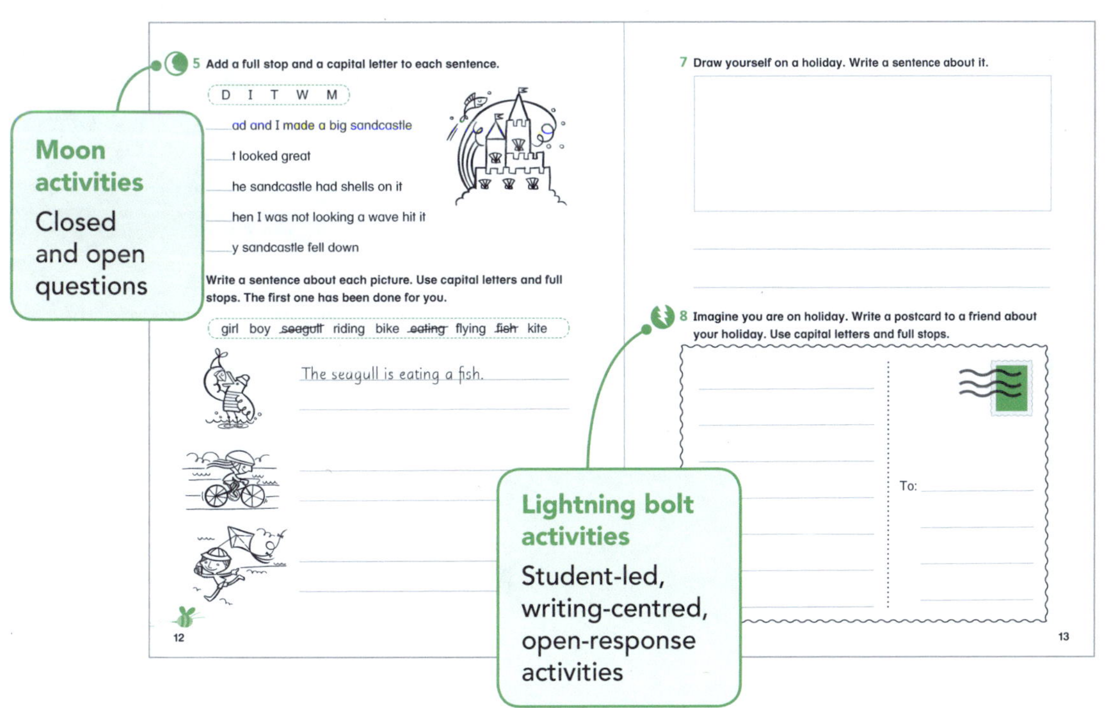

5 Add a full stop and a capital letter to each sentence.

D I T W M

___ad and I made a big sandcastle
___t looked great
___he sandcastle had shells on it
___hen I was not looking a wave hit it
___y sandcastle fell down

6 Write a sentence about each picture. Use capital letters and full stops. The first one has been done for you.

girl boy ~~seagull~~ riding bike ~~eating~~ flying ~~fish~~ kite

The seagull is eating a fish.

12

7 Draw yourself on a holiday. Write a sentence about it.

8 Imagine you are on holiday. Write a postcard to a friend about your holiday. Use capital letters and full stops.

To:

13

Lightning bolt activities
Student-led, writing-centred, open-response activities

Scope and Sequence

Unit	Unit title	Page	Text / text type	Text and sentence grammar skill	Word level grammar skill	Focus on
1	**My Holiday**	10	Postcard	Simple sentences	Capital letters Full stops	Capitals at the beginning of sentences and full stops at the end
2	**A Frog's Life Cycle**	14	Information report	Statements of fact	Common nouns	E.g. boy, frog, water, house
3	**The Rainforest**	18	Poem	Descriptive sentences	Adjectives	E.g. tall, green, fast, happy
4	**Strawberry Patch**	22	Instructions	Present tense	Verbs – present tense	E.g. cover, put, place, cut
5	**Life in Beijing**	26	Information report	Statements	Capital letters Full stops	Revise capitals at the beginning of sentences and full stops at the end
6	**Happy New Year!**	30	Personal recount	Past tense	Verbs – past tense	E.g. went, saw, walked, ate, liked
7	**100 Goals**	34	Historical recount	Statements of fact	Action verbs	E.g. cheered, kicked, jumped
8	**Crocodile Tour**	38	Journal	Indirect speech	Personal pronouns	E.g. I, you, he, she

	Australian Curriculum content descriptions*	General capabilities / cross-curriculum priorities*	Learning areas*
	Recognise that different types of punctuation, including full stops, question marks and exclamation marks, signal sentences that make statements, ask questions, express emotion or give commands (*ACELA1449*) Also: *ACELA1451, ACELY1661*	• Literacy • Critical and creative thinking	English
	Explore differences in words that represent people, places and things (nouns and pronouns), actions (verbs), qualities (adjectives) and details like when, where and how (adverbs) (*ACELA1452*) Also: *ACELA1451, ACELA1447*	• Literacy • Critical and creative thinking	English Science
	Create short imaginative and informative texts that show emerging use of appropriate text structure, sentence-level grammar, word choice, spelling, punctuation and appropriate multimodal elements, for example illustrations and diagrams (*ACELY1661*) Also: *ACELA1452, ACELY1658*	• Literacy • Critical and creative thinking • Sustainability	English Science
	Explore differences in words that represent people, places and things (nouns and pronouns), actions (verbs), qualities (adjectives) and details like when, where and how (adverbs) (*ACELA1452*) Also: *ACELA1447, ACELA1453*	• Literacy • Critical and creative thinking • Sustainability	English Maths
	Recognise that different types of punctuation, including full stops, question marks and exclamation marks, signal sentences that make statements, ask questions, express emotion or give commands (*ACELA1449*) Also: *ACELA1451, ACELY1661*	• Literacy • Critical and creative thinking • Intercultural understanding • Asia and Australia's engagement with Asia	English Geography
	Explore differences in words that represent people, places and things (nouns and pronouns), actions (verbs), qualities (adjectives) and details like when, where and how (adverbs) (*ACELA1452*) Also: *ACELA1447, ACELA1453*	• Literacy • Critical and creative thinking • Intercultural understanding • Asia and Australia's engagement with Asia	English
	Identify the parts of a simple sentence that represent 'What's happening?', 'Who or what is doing or receiving the action?' and the circumstances surrounding the action (*ACELA1451*) Also: *ACELA1452, ACELY1658*	• Literacy • Critical and creative thinking • Intercultural understanding • Aboriginal and Torres Strait Islander histories and cultures	English History
	Explore differences in words that represent people, places and things (nouns and pronouns), actions (verbs), qualities (adjectives) and details like when, where and how (adverbs) (*ACELA1452*) Also: *ACELA1451, ACELY1658*	• Literacy • Critical and creative thinking • Intercultural understanding • Aboriginal and Torres Strait Islander histories and cultures	English Geography

****Source:*** *Australian Curriculum*

Unit	Unit title	Page	Text / text type	Text and sentence grammar skill	Word level grammar skill	Focus on
9	**Transport**	42	Concept map	Simple sentences	Compound words	E.g. tugboat, airport, skateboard
10	**You Are Invited**	46	Invitation	Precise language	Proper nouns	E.g. Luke, Lilly, Sydney, Brisbane
11	**Don't Drop Rubbish!**	50	Poem	Emotive language	Exclamation marks	E.g. We hate rubbish!
12	**What Do Ants Eat?**	54	Information report	Questioning	Question marks	E.g. Where do ants live?
13	**Jack and the Beanstalk**	58	Fairytale	Direct speech	Common nouns Proper nouns	E.g. Jack, boy
14	**Fruit Rockets**	62	Recipe	Commands	Number adjectives	E.g. one banana, two oranges
15	**Ant's New Nest**	66	Narrative	Descriptive sentences	Adverbs	E.g. quickly, rarely, slowly, here, often, everywhere
16	**Dear Diary**	70	Diary	Simple sentences	Capital letters Proper nouns	Capitals for names and places

	Australian Curriculum content descriptions*	General capabilities / cross-curriculum priorities*	Learning areas*
	Identify the parts of a simple sentence that represent 'What's happening?', 'Who or what is doing or receiving the action?' and the circumstances surrounding the action (*ACELA1451*) Also: *ACELA1449, ACELA1452*	• Literacy • Critical and creative thinking • ICT competence	English
	Understand the use of vocabulary in everyday contexts as well as a growing number of school contexts, including appropriate use of formal and informal terms of address in different contexts (*ACELA1454*) Also: *ACELA1452, ACELA1451*	• Literacy • Critical and creative thinking • Personal and social competence • Numeracy	English Maths
	Recognise that different types of punctuation, including full stops, question marks and exclamation marks, signal sentences that make statements, ask questions, express emotion or give commands (*ACELA1449*) Also: *ACELA1585, ACELY1661*	• Literacy • Critical and creative thinking • Personal and social competence • Ethical behaviour • Sustainability	English
	Understand that there are different ways of asking for information, making offers and giving commands (*ACELA1446*) Also: *ACELA1449, ACELA1447*	• Literacy • Critical and creative thinking • ICT competence	English Science
	Explore differences in words that represent people, places and things (nouns and pronouns), actions (verbs), qualities (adjectives) and details like when, where and how (adverbs) (*ACELA1452*) Also: *ACELA1452, ACELA1451*	• Literacy • Critical and creative thinking	English
	Understand that there are different ways of asking for information, making offers and giving commands (*ACELA1446*) Also: *ACELA1449, ACELA1452*	• Literacy • Critical and creative thinking • Personal and social competence • Numeracy	English Maths
	Explore differences in words that represent people, places and things (nouns and pronouns), actions (verbs), qualities (adjectives) and details like when, where and how (adverbs) (*ACELA1452*) Also: *ACELA1453, ACELY1661*	• Literacy • Critical and creative thinking • Personal and social competence	English
	Explore differences in words that represent people, places and things (nouns and pronouns), actions (verbs), qualities (adjectives) and details like when, where and how (adverbs) (*ACELA1452*) Also: *ACELA1449, ACELA1453*	• Literacy • Critical and creative thinking • Numeracy	English Maths

***Source:** *Australian Curriculum*

Unit	Unit title	Page	Text / text type	Text and sentence grammar skill	Word level grammar skill	Focus on
17	**Scooter for Sale!**	74	Advertisement	Emotive language	Exclamation marks	Exclamations
18	**Birds of Prey**	78	Explanation	Simple sentences	Action verbs Adverbs	Verbs: shines, turns, moves Adverbs: brightly, gently, slowly
19	**Around Australia**	82	Recount	Past tense	Capital letters Proper nouns	Revising capital letters for place names
20	**Princess Polly**	86	Poem	Patterns of repetition	Words with the same initial sound (alliteration)	E.g. pretty princess; creepy, cold, castle
21	**Day and Night**	90	Explanation	Questioning	Question marks	E.g. What is day and night?
22	**What a Party!**	94	Thank-you letter	Formal language	Personal pronouns	Revising I, you, he, she
23	**Treasure Map**	98	Directions	Commands	Prepositions	E.g. around, over, in, on, up, with
24	**Super Gran!**	102	Comic strip	Informal language	Action verbs	E.g. jump, fly, grab
25	**Super Gran Again**	106	Narrative	Present tense	Adjectives	E.g. sweet, old, cheeky

	Australian Curriculum content descriptions*	General capabilities / cross-curriculum priorities*	Learning areas*
	Recognise that different types of punctuation, including full stops, question marks and exclamation marks, signal sentences that make statements, ask questions, express emotion or give commands (*ACELA1449*) Also: *ACELA1452, ACELA1447*	• Literacy • Critical and creative thinking • Numeracy	English Maths
	Explore differences in words that represent people, places and things (nouns and pronouns), actions (verbs), qualities (adjectives) and details like when, where and how (adverbs) (*ACELA1452*) Also: *ACELA1451, ACELA1454*	• Literacy • Critical and creative thinking	English Science
	Recognise that different types of punctuation, including full stops, question marks and exclamation marks, signal sentences that make statements, ask questions, express emotion or give commands (*ACELA1449*) Also: *ACELY1658, ACELA1452*	• Literacy • Critical and creative thinking • ICT competence	English Geography
	Understand patterns of repetition and contrast in simple texts (*ACELA1448*) Also: *ACELT1585, ACELA1454*	• Literacy • Critical and creative thinking	English
	Recognise that different types of punctuation, including full stops, question marks and exclamation marks, signal sentences that make statements, ask questions, express emotion or give commands (*ACELA1449*) Also: *ACELY1661, ACELA1446*	• Literacy • Critical and creative thinking	English Science
	Understand the use of vocabulary in everyday contexts as well as a growing number of school contexts, including appropriate use of formal and informal terms of address in different contexts (*ACELA1454*) Also: *ACELA1452, ACELA1447*	• Literacy • Critical and creative thinking • Numeracy	English Maths
	Explore differences in words that represent people, places and things (nouns and pronouns), actions (verbs), qualities (adjectives) and details like when, where and how (adverbs) (*ACELA1452*) Also: *ACELA1447, ACELA1446*	• Literacy • Critical and creative thinking • Numeracy	English Maths
	Understand the use of vocabulary in everyday contexts as well as a growing number of school contexts, including appropriate use of formal and informal terms of address in different contexts (*ACELA1454*) Also: *ACELA1451, ACELA1452*	• Literacy • Critical and creative thinking	English
	Explore differences in words that represent people, places and things (nouns and pronouns), actions (verbs), qualities (adjectives) and details like when, where and how (adverbs) (*ACELA1452*) Also: *ACELY1661, ACELY1658*	• Literacy • Critical and creative thinking	English

**Source:* *Australian Curriculum*

Unit 1

My Holiday

A **simple sentence** is a group of words about a single idea. *I went to the beach.*

A **capital letter** is used at the start of a sentence.
A **full stop** is used at the end of a sentence.
My holiday was fun.

Postcard

Dear Grandma,

I am on holiday at the beach. It is very hot!

Dad and I went swimming in the sea.
Then I made a big sandcastle.

We also went to the zoo. We saw a lot of animals. There was a baby elephant.

I am having fun on my holiday.

Love,

Harry.

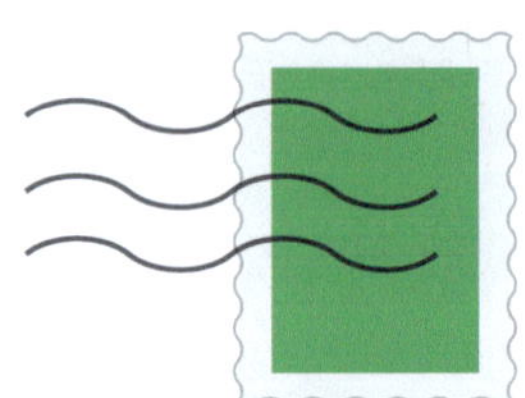

To: Ruth Fraser
5 Penny Lane
Redcliffe 4020

1 **Trace the capital letters in the postcard.**

2 **Circle the full stops in the postcard.**

3 Add a full stop to these sentences.

The boy went swimming in the sea

The girl made a sandcastle

It was very big

The boy walked on the sand

He found a crab

4 Trace the capital letter at the start of each sentence.

On our holidays, we went to the beach.

It was very hot.

We built a sandcastle.

The waves were big.

My holiday was fun.

5 Add a full stop and a capital letter to each sentence.

D I T W M

____ad and I made a big sandcastle

____t looked great

____he sandcastle had shells on it

____hen I was not looking a wave hit it

____y sandcastle fell down

6 Write a sentence about each picture. Use capital letters and full stops. The first one has been done for you.

girl boy ~~seagull~~ riding bike ~~eating~~ flying ~~fish~~ kite

The seagull is eating a fish.

____

____

____

____

____

7 **Draw yourself on a holiday. Write a sentence about it.**

8 **Imagine you are on holiday. Write a postcard to a friend about your holiday. Use capital letters and full stops.**

To:

Unit 2 A Frog's Life Cycle

A **noun** is a word that names people, places and things.
A **common noun** names general groups of things.
Student, *park*, *frog* and *water* are common nouns.
A sentence that states a fact is a **statement**.
Frogs lay eggs.

Information Report

A Frog's Life Cycle

The life cycle of a frog is very interesting.

Frogs lay eggs in water.

The eggs hatch into tadpoles.

The tadpoles live in the water.

As the tadpoles grow, they start to turn into frogs.

They grow legs and lungs.

They lose their tails.

They are now frogs!

Frogs can live on land and in water.

1 **Trace the circles around five nouns in the information report. Circle five more nouns.**

2 **Write three nouns from the information report.**

______________ ______________ ______________

3 **Circle all the nouns.**

grow tadpoles turn frogs start

water lay tail eggs legs

4 **Draw a line from the statement to its picture.**

Tadpoles live in the water.

Frogs can live on land.

Frogs lay eggs in the water.

5 **Write five nouns from the picture.**

____

____

____

____

____

6 **Write each noun in its correct group. Add two more nouns to each group.**

lake frog Tom zoo pencil
Lucy baby beach table

People	Places	Things

7 **Circle the nouns in the sentence.**

Frogs' eggs hatch into tadpoles.

Bicycles have two wheels.

Insects have six legs.

Kittens grow into cats.

8 Write an information report about an animal you know.

An information report about ____________________

Unit 3

The Rainforest

An **adjective** is a word that describes a noun. *Tall*, *green*, *fast* and *happy* are all adjectives. Sentences that use many adjectives are called **descriptive sentences**. *The bird sat in a tall tree.*

Poem

The Rainforest

Water runs over smooth rocks,
thick vines hang from tall trees.
new, green plants grow.
Rainforest.

Colourful birds fly from tree to tree,
green frogs croak,
small beetles hide on the forest floor.
Rainforest.

Cool, damp forest air,
living forest, growing forest,
we must look after you.
Rainforest.

1 **Trace the lines under five adjectives in the poem. Underline five more.**

2 **Circle the adjectives.**

small beetle

green frog

tall trees

colourful birds

3 **Write the adjective used in the poem to describe the noun.**

________________ rocks

________________ vines

________________ birds

4 **Tick the sentence that is more descriptive.**

Thick vines hang from tall trees.

Vines hang from trees.

5 **Write a descriptive sentence about each picture. Remember to use adjectives.**

____

____

6 Write an adjective to describe each animal. Use the words in the box.

spotty	long	happy	fat	cute	fierce	stripy	tiny

 7 **Write five descriptive sentences about a place you love to visit. Use as many adjectives as you can.**

I love to visit ______________________________.

Unit 4 Strawberry Patch

A **verb** is word that tells what someone or something is doing. *The mouse is sleeping.*

The **tense** of a verb shows when it happened.

A **present tense verb** shows what is happening now.

Instructions

How to make a strawberry patch

You will need:

- 4 pieces of wood
- soil
- black plastic
- scissors
- 6 small strawberry plants
- a watering can

What to do:

1 Make a square with the four pieces of wood.

2 Fill the square with the soil.

3 Cover the soil with the black plastic.

4 Ask an adult to cut six small holes in the plastic.

5 Put each strawberry plant through a hole, into the soil.

6 Water the strawberry plants!

1 **Trace the line under the verbs in the instructions.**

2 **Write three verbs from the instructions.**

3 **Write down a present tense verb for each picture:**

4 **Draw a picture for each verb.**

dig	**grow**

5 **Circle the present tense verbs below.**

kick sing jumped shout
swim kicked ran
hopped run mix
sang dreamed

6 **Number the steps in the right order from 1 to 4. Then circle the verbs.**

_____ Put the seed in the hole.

_____ Water the seed.

_____ Dig a hole in the soil.

_____ Fill the pot with soil.

7 **Write the correct verb for each picture.**

pour swim hammer kick

_______________ _______________

_______________ _______________

8 Write a procedure about how to make or do something. You could explain how to make a sandwich, play a game or build a sandcastle.

How to make ____________

You will need:

- ____________
- ____________
- ____________
- ____________

What to do:

1 ____________

2 ____________

3 ____________

4 ____________

5 ____________

6 ____________

9 Write the verbs you used in your procedure.

____________ ____________ ____________

____________ ____________ ____________

Unit 5 Life in Beijing

A sentence that states a fact is a **statement**.

Beijing is a city in China.

A **capital letter** is used at the start of a statement.

A **full stop** is used at the end of a statement.

The capital of China is Beijing.

Information Report

Life in Beijing

Beijing is the capital city of China.

Over 22 million people live in Beijing.

It is a very crowded city.

The streets in Beijing are always busy.

There are lots of cars, buses and bikes.

There are also lots of big stores, shops and markets.

1 Trace the capital letters in the information report.

2 Circle all the full stops in the information report.

3 **Add full stops to each statement below. Then, circle the capital letters at the start of each statement.**

China's flag is red and yellow

The giant panda is native to China

4 **Rewrite the statements correctly. Use capital letters and full stops.**

beijing is a very crowded city

___

the streets in Beijing are always busy

___

5 **Tick all the sentences that are statements. Remember, a statement is a sentence that gives a fact or opinion.**

What time do we leave for the circus?

The capital city of China is Beijing.

I am six years old.

Where is my new blue coat?

My father's name is Wei Long.

6 Write a statement about Beijing. Use your own words.

7 Write a statement for each picture.

8 What is the rule for using full stops?

 9 Where do you live? Write an information report about your city or town. Then draw a picture.

Life in ______________________

Unit 6 Happy New Year!

A **verb** is word that tells what someone or something is doing.

The **tense** of a verb shows when it happened.

A **past tense verb** shows what was being done in the past. *The dog barked last night.*

Personal Recount

Happy Chinese New Year!

On Sunday, Dad and I went to a Chinese New Year festival. First, we watched the parade. The Chinese acrobats jumped and danced. People banged big drums.

We saw a Chinese dragon, too!

Then Dad and I watched a dragon boat race. That night, we watched the fireworks. They flew up into the sky!

I loved the Chinese New Year festival!

1 **Trace the line under the past tense verbs in the personal recount.**

2 **Write three past tense verbs from the personal recount.**

__________ __________ __________

3 **Add a past tense verb to each sentence.**

flew watched banged

First, we __________ the parade.

People __________ big drums.

They __________ up into the sky!

4 **Draw lines to match each past tense verb to a picture.**

shouted

barked

danced

ate

5 **Choose a verb from question 4. Use the verb in a sentence.**

____

____

6 Circle the past tense verbs.

We ate fried rice.

She patted the kitten.

We went to the zoo.

I ran around the park.

7 Fill the gap with a past tense verb. Use the words in the box.

jumped rode ate hugged

The girl _______________ her scooter.

The dancer _______________ up high.

The boy _______________ his teddy bear.

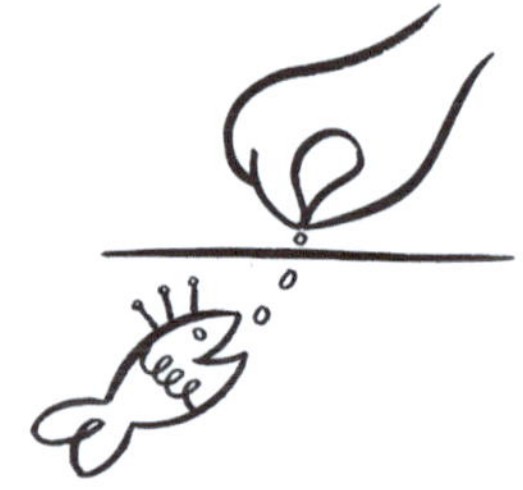

The fish _______________ its food.

8 Write some more past tense verbs in the box.

9 Write about a party you have been to. Then draw a picture.

Unit 7 100 Goals

An **action verb** is a word that shows what is being done. It is a "doing" word. *The man ran fast.*

A sentence that states a fact is a **statement**.

Buddy Franklin is a football player.

Historical Recount

Buddy Franklin Kicks 100 Goals!

Buddy Franklin is an AFL football player. He plays for Hawthorn. In 2008, he won a special medal for kicking the most goals in the season.

Buddy and his team were playing Carlton when he kicked his 100th goal! The crowd clapped and cheered. Lots of people ran onto the oval. They patted Buddy on the back. Buddy was the first Indigenous Australian player to kick 100 goals in a season.

Well done, Buddy!

1 **Trace the action verbs in the historical recount.**

2 **Write three action verbs from the historical recount.**

______________ ______________ ______________

3 **Draw a line to match the action verb to a picture.**

kicked clapped ran

4 **Fill the gap with an action verb.**

Buddy ______________ 100 goals.

The crowd ______________ and cheered.

They ______________ Buddy on the back.

5 **Write the action verb from each group of words.**

clap ball the boy ______________

grass run tigers it ______________

cats small jump fast ______________

6 Underline the action verbs.

Tennis players hit tennis balls.

An Olympic swimmer swims fast.

AFL players kick and mark footballs.

7 Write three statements about the picture.

8 **Write three action verbs for washing your teeth. The first one has been done for you.**

squeeze ______ ______

9 **Write about your favourite sportsperson or team. Then draw a picture.**

Unit 8

Crocodile Tour

A **personal pronoun** takes the place of a noun. *<u>Jane</u> went on a crocodile tour. <u>She</u> went on a crocodile tour.*

Indirect speech tells what someone has said but does not use their exact words. *Matt said that crocodiles were his favourite animals.*

Journal

Saturday 14 August

Today, Mum, Dad and I went on a crocodile tour. We went on a boat on the Daintree River in Queensland. Matt was our tour guide. He was an Aboriginal Australian. He told me he loves spotting big crocodiles.

We went down the river. Matt yelled out that he saw a croc! Mum saw the crocodile before I did. She pointed to it. It was a huge adult crocodile. Matt said its name was Fat Albert.

1 **Trace the circles around the pronouns in the journal.**

2 **Copy a sentence from the journal that has a pronoun. Circle the pronoun.**

3 **Underline the pronouns in the sentences.**

We went on a boat on the Daintree River.

He moved the boat closer to the river bank.

It was a tiny baby crocodile.

I think the croc tour was the best part of the holiday.

4 **Underline a sentence in the journal that uses indirect speech.**

Hint: Matt yelled out that he saw a croc!

5 **Draw a line to match the words with the correct pronoun.**

Grandma and Grandpa	it
Matt	they
the boat	she
Mum	he

6 Rewrite each sentence. Use a pronoun in place of the underlined words.

he she it they

Ben fed his cat.

Emma and Kate went to the shop.

The bike was new and shiny.

Ling fixed her bike.

---

7 Draw a smiley face beside the sentence that uses indirect speech.

"His name is Fat Albert," said Matt.

Matt said his name was Fat Albert.

8 Write the pronouns in the correct place.

we they he me you them us her him

Singular pronouns (one person or thing)	Plural pronouns (more than one person or thing)

9 Write a journal entry about an exciting place you have been. Remember to include some pronouns.

Unit 9 Transport

A **compound word** is a word made from two smaller words. *Railway* is made from *rail* and *way*.

A **simple sentence** is a group of words about a single idea. *The truck is red.*

Concept Map

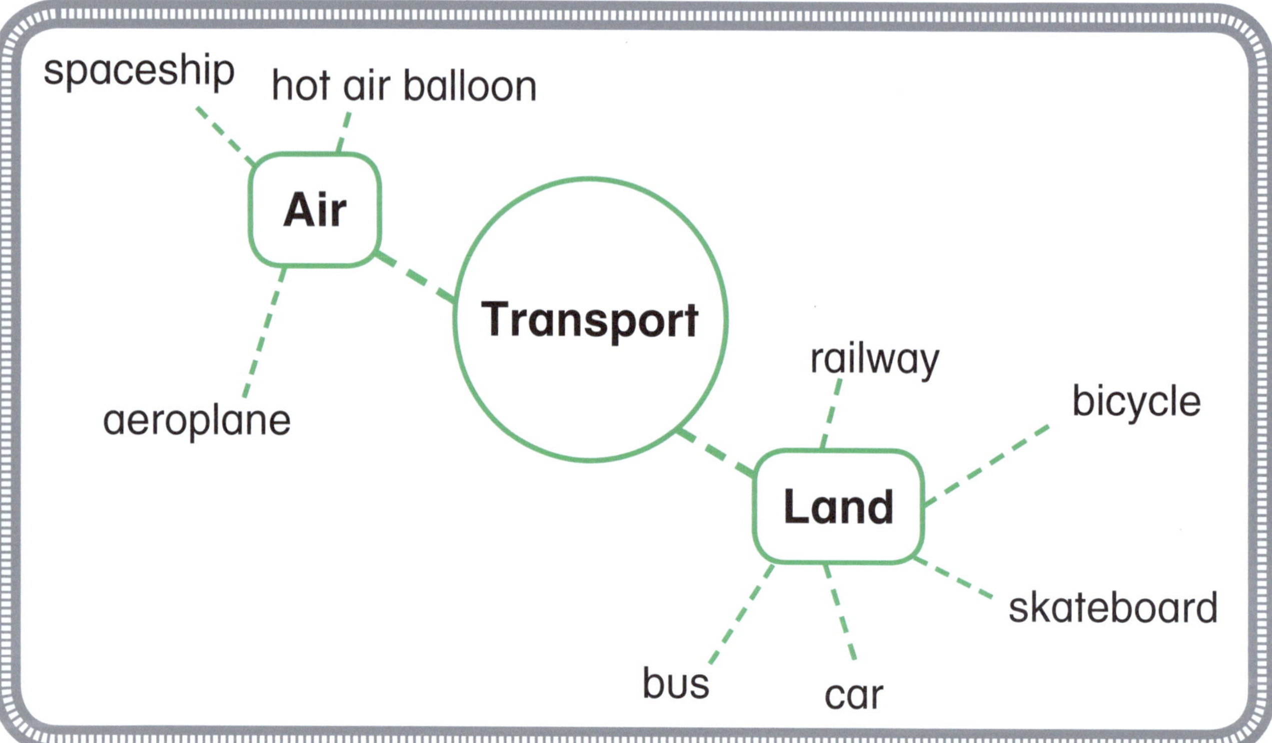

1 Circle these compound words in the concept map.

spaceship skateboard railway

2 Write three ways to travel on land.

_______________ _______________ _______________

3 **Draw a line to join two words to make a compound word.**

space	board
wheel	ship
tug	chair
skate	boat

4 **Tick the simple sentence. Remember, a simple sentence is about one idea.**

My book was in the bookcase.

My book was on the floor because the bookcase was full.

5 **Split these compound words into two words.**

rollerblade roller and blade

airport ______ and ______

hovercraft ______ and ______

wheelchair ______ and ______

railway ______ and ______

6 **Make a compound word for each picture. Use the words in the box.**

foot fly gold butter bow rain fish ball

7 **Circle the compound word in each sentence.**
Draw a picture of one circled word.

Cara got sunburnt.

Dad reads the newspaper.

I said goodbye to Mum.

She is a firefighter.

The seaweed is green.

Polly fell off the snowboard.

My birthday is soon.

8 **Draw a smiley face beside the simple sentence.**

The tractor is blue.

The tractor is blue on one side and brown on the other, with two pink doors.

9 **Write a simple sentence about each compound word.**

birthday

sunburnt

railway

butterfly

10 **Go online to find out more about butterflies.**

Unit 10 You Are Invited

Proper nouns are the names of individual people, places and things. Proper nouns always have a **capital letter**.

Precise language is language that uses words that are clear and to the point.

Invitation

Dear Patrick,

You are invited to Luke's 7th birthday party.

When: Saturday 15 October

Time: 1.00 pm – 4.00 pm

Where: Fun Land
12 Celebration Road
Merryville

Dress as your favourite superhero.

RSVP: Call Sharon on 0400 377 773

1 **Trace the lines under three proper nouns in the invitation. Underline three more.**

2 **Circle all the proper nouns.**

Luke	party	superhero	October
invitation	Sharon	Saturday	Merryville

3 **Write the proper nouns with their capital letters.**

luke ____________

fun land ____________

sharon ____________

4 **Tick the sentence that uses precise language. Remember, precise language is clear and to the point.**

Please sit in the car.

Maybe we can get in the car in a little while.

5 **Circle all the proper nouns in the sentences.**

I live in a house on Long Street.

Sally was going to a party.

My teacher is Mr Lee.

The dog barked at Zac.

6 **Write the nouns in their correct group. The first one has been done for you.**

Zac dog teacher Mr Lee party
~~Long Street~~ ~~house~~ Sally

Common nouns	Proper nouns
house	Long Street

7 **Write a proper noun for the words that are underlined.**

I played with <u>my sister</u>.

I played with ____________________.

I told my friend a joke.

I told ________________ a joke.

The party is tomorrow.

The party is on ________________.

 **8 Write your own party invitation. Circle your proper nouns.**

Unit 11 Don't Drop Rubbish!

An **exclamation** is a sentence that shows a strong feeling. An exclamation ends with an **exclamation mark**. *Do not drop rubbish!*
An exclamation often uses emotive language.
Emotive language uses words that make us feel something.

Poem

Don't Drop Rubbish!

No rubbish on the ground.
We love our fresh air.
Plants are dying! Rivers are brown!
Rubbish is all around.

Stop it!
Don't drop it!

Clean air! Clean water!
We hate rubbish on the ground.
Plants are growing. Rivers are running.
No rubbish is to be found.

We can do it!
Don't drop it!

1 **Circle all the exclamation marks in the poem.**

2 **Write some exclamation marks on the line.**

! !

3 **Underline these emotive words in the poem.**

love hate

4 **Circle the exclamations.**

Rubbish on the ground.

Stop it!

We can do it!

Plants are growing.

We need clean water!

Don't drop it!

5 **Draw a picture of something that makes you laugh. Write a sentence about your picture. Use emotive words.**

6 **Draw a line to match the exclamation to a picture.**

I'm cold!

Slow down!

Nice car!

Don't drop it!

7 **Write an exclamation about this picture.**

---

8 **Draw a smiley face beside the sentence in each pair that uses emotive language. Remember, emotive language uses words that make us feel something.**

There is some rubbish.
Yuk! I hate that dirty rubbish.

I am sacred to ride my bike down the big hill.
I am riding a bike.

The baby bird wants food.
The baby bird is crying for its dinner.

9 Write about a time you were happy. Use emotive language.

10 Write about a time you were sad. Use emotive language.

11 Go on the internet to learn about Clean Up Australia Day.

Unit 12 What Do Ants Eat?

A **question** is a sentence that asks something.

Where do ants live?

A question always ends with a **question mark**.

What do ants eat?

Information Report

Ants

Ants are small insects.

Where do ants live?

Ants live in groups called colonies.

They build nests to live in.

What do ants look like?

Ants have six legs.

They have two antennae on their head.

They use the antennae to smell, taste and hear.

Ants can be lots of colours, such as red, black and green.

What do ants eat?

Ants can eat human food, plants and other insects.

Some ants even eat wood!

1 **Underline all the questions in the information report.**

2 **Circle all the question marks in the information report.**

3 **Write some question marks on the line.**

? ?

4 **Add question marks to these questions.**

Where do ants live

What do ants look like

What do ants eat

How many legs do ants have

Can ants be lots of colours

Do some ants eat wood

5 **Draw a line to match each picture to a question.**

What does a lion look like?

How many legs does an ant have?

Do spiders spin webs?

6 **Write a question about each picture.**

7 **Write a question for the answer below.**

Question:

Answer:

My cat Simba sleeps on a chair by the fire.

8 **Write an information report with questions and answers about one of these animals. Use the internet to help you.**

Unit 13 Jack and the Beanstalk

Direct speech is what someone says. Direct speech uses **quotation marks**. They are placed around what is being said. *"I have a pet cow," said Jack.*

Common and proper nouns are used for people, places and things. Proper nouns always have a capital letter.

Fairytale

Once upon a time, there was a boy called Jack. Jack and his mother were very poor. All they had was a cow.

"Jack!" said his mother. "Take our cow to the market and sell her."

On the way to the market, Jack met a man.

"I will give you five magic beans for your cow," said the man.

"Okay!" said Jack.

Jack showed his mother the magic beans.

"You silly boy!" she yelled. She threw the beans outside.

The next morning, Jack looked outside.

"Wow!" said Jack.

The beans had grown into a giant beanstalk!

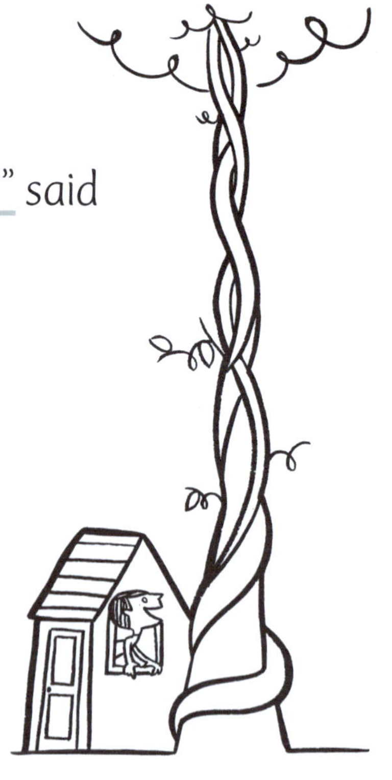

1 **Trace the lines under the direct speech in the fairytale.**

2 **Circle all the quotation marks in the fairytale.**

3 **Write quotation marks around the word *Hello*. The first one has been done for you.**

"Hello" Hello Hello Hello Hello Hello

4 **Draw a line to match the direct speech to a character from the fairytale.**

"You silly boy!"

"Okay!"

"I will give you five magic beans for your cow."

5 **Write a P beside the proper nouns and a C beside the common nouns.**

Jack	______	school	______
boy	______	dog	______
Cinderella	______	Max	______
girl	______	beans	______

6 **Write some direct speech for the cow. Remember to use quotation marks.**

____

____

7 **Draw what you think is at the top of the beanstalk.**

8 **Rewrite these sentences with a different proper noun.**

My favourite city is <u>Melbourne</u>.

____

I wish my name was <u>Laura</u>.

____

<u>Mr Smith</u> owns the lolly shop.

____

9 Fill the gaps with the correct common or proper noun.

kite   Baxter   Darwin   carrots

I live in a city called ______________.

Taj has a dog called ______________.

Baxter

I love to fly my ______________.

My favourite vegetables are ______________.

10 Write about your favourite fairytale. Use some direct speech to show what one character says to another.

____

____

____

____

____

____

____

Unit 14 Fruit Rockets

A **number adjective** shows how many of something there is. *You will need four grapes.* A number adjective can also show the order of things. *Put the first grape on the skewer.*

A sentence that tells us what to do is a **command**.
Peel the banana.

Recipe

Fruit Rockets

You will need:

- 1 peeled banana
- 2 pieces of watermelon
- 4 grapes
- 4 strawberries
- 1 stick

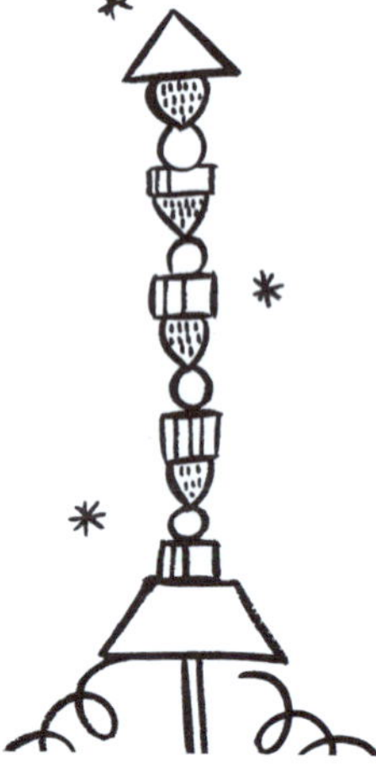

What to do:

1 Ask an adult to cut the banana into four pieces.

2 Put the first piece of watermelon on the stick.

3 Put one banana piece onto the stick.

4 Put one grape onto the stick.

5 Put one strawberry onto the stick.

6 Do steps 3–5 three more times.

7 Put the second piece of watermelon onto the end of the stick.

8 Eat your Fruit Rocket. Yum!

1 **Trace the number adjectives in the recipe.**

2 **Write a command from the recipe.**

____

3 **Write the number adjective. Use the picture to help you.**

__________ grapes

__________ strawberries

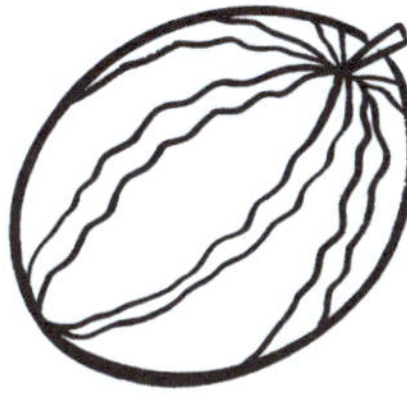

__________ watermelon

4 **Draw a line to match each picture to a command. Underline all the number adjectives.**

Peel two bananas.

Pick up one card.

Turn left at the stop sign.

5 **Write your own command for the dog in the picture.**

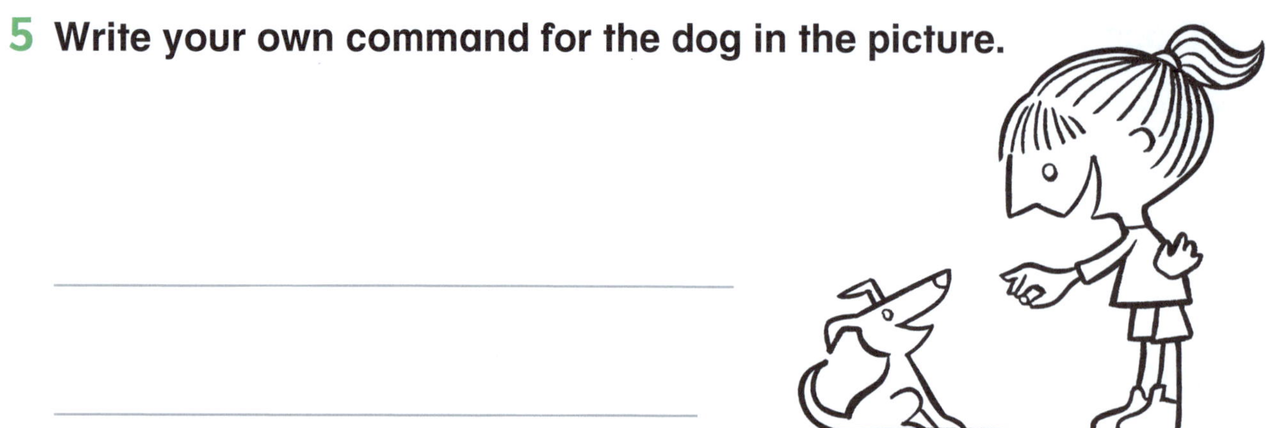

6 **Write the correct number adjective in the boxes.**

first second third

7 **Draw a smiley face next to each sentence that is a command. Remember, commands tell us to do something.**

Clean your room before dinner.

Can I go outside before dinner?

Wave goodbye to your friend.

Is my friend waving?

8 **Circle the number adjective in each sentence.**

There were three children in the race.

The second child to cross the line had black hair.

9 **How do we brush our teeth? Write a procedure about how to brush your teeth. Use some commands and number adjectives.**

You will need:

- ____________________
- ____________________
- ____________________
- ____________________

What to do:

First, squeeze some toothpaste onto your brush.

Unit 15 Ant's New Nest

An **adverb** adds information to a verb. It shows when, where or how the action happens. *Ant ate yesterday.*

Descriptive sentences describe something. They often use adverbs. *Ant bravely climbed over the log.*

Narrative

Ant's New Nest

Ant was busily searching for food. When it was time to go home, she couldn't find her nest.

"I am lost," said Ant sadly. "I must find my nest quickly."

Ant found a tin can and carefully looked inside.

"Get out!" said Spider loudly. "I live here."

Ant bravely climbed up a drainpipe. Bird was at the top.

"This is not your nest!" Bird said crossly.

At last she saw some other ants walking quickly to their nest.

"I will follow them," Ant said excitedly. She was not lost anymore!

1 **Trace the circles around the adverbs in the narrative. Circle five more.**

2 **Draw a line to match what Ant did (the verb) to how Ant did it (the adverb).**

Ant looked	carefully
Ant said	bravely
Ant climbed	excitedly

3 **Tick the descriptive sentence.**

Kate gently put the small spider in the long grass.

Kate put the spider in the grass.

4 **Fill the gaps with an adverb.**

quickly slowly sadly loudly quietly

Ant walked ________________ home.

The sick baby cried ________________.

The boy read his comic book ________________.

5 **Write a descriptive sentence about each picture. Use an adverb in each sentence.**

____

____

____

____

____

____

6 **Write the adverb to describe how you speak.**

loudly softly

When the baby is sleeping, I speak ______________.

When I'm in the noisy playground, I speak ______________.

7 **Circle the adverbs in each descriptive sentence.**

Kim walked slowly home.

She ate quickly.

The lady sang loudly.

The baby slept softly.

The boy jumped bravely.

8 Write three descriptive sentences about the picture. Use adverbs to say when, where and how the things happen.

Unit 16 Dear Diary

Proper nouns are the names of people, places and things. Proper nouns always have a **capital letter**.

Lucy went to Riverton in July.

A **simple sentence** makes sense by itself and is about a single idea. *We went to the lake.*

Diary

Friday 15 March

Today we went on a school trip. We went to Lake King. It was a lot of fun.

Tracey was our guide. She told us about the animals that live near the lake.

Tomorrow I am going to visit my cousin Lucy. Lucy and Aunty Jane live in Robe. I can't wait to see them!

Saturday 16 March

Lucy and I had so much fun today. We went to the Port Peel Market. I bought a toy for baby Zac. We had lunch at a cafe called Fay's Fresh Foods. It was yummy!

1 **Trace the lines under the proper nouns in the diary.**

2 **Write two proper nouns from the diary that are the names of people.**

________________ ________________

3 **Write two proper nouns from the diary that are the names of places.**

4 **Copy a simple sentence from the diary.**

5 **Rewrite each sentence. Make sure you use capital letters.**

we went to lake king.

tracey was our guide.

we went to the port peel market.

6 **Write the proper nouns in the correct column.**

Uluru Tasmania Mr Watson Jenny Pete China

Names of people	Names of places

7 **The writer has forgotten to use capital letters for proper nouns. Circle the letters that should be capitals.**

Sunday 17 March

Today, lucy, aunty jane and I went to a place called beachport. We met anita and nisha. We went swimming at the beach. Tomorrow, I have to go to school. I wonder what mr watson did on his weekend?

8 **Answer each question with a simple sentence.**

What is your name?

____

Where do you live?

____

What is a place you would like to visit?

What is the name of your pet (or a friend's pet)?

9 What did you do last Saturday? Write a diary entry about it. Use capital letters for the proper nouns.

Unit 17

Scooter for Sale!

An **exclamation** is a sentence that shows a strong feeling. It ends with an **exclamation mark**. *Do not miss the bus!*

An exclamation often uses emotive language.

Emotive language uses words that make us feel something. *How exciting!*

Advertisement

Scooter for Sale!

Awesome green scooter for sale.

Only $30.00!

Perfect for boys or girls, ages 5+

Only 6 months old. Looks brand new!

- movable handlebars
- rear brake
- can be folded up

How exciting!

Don't miss out! Sad to sell!

Call Alex on 0438SCOOTA.

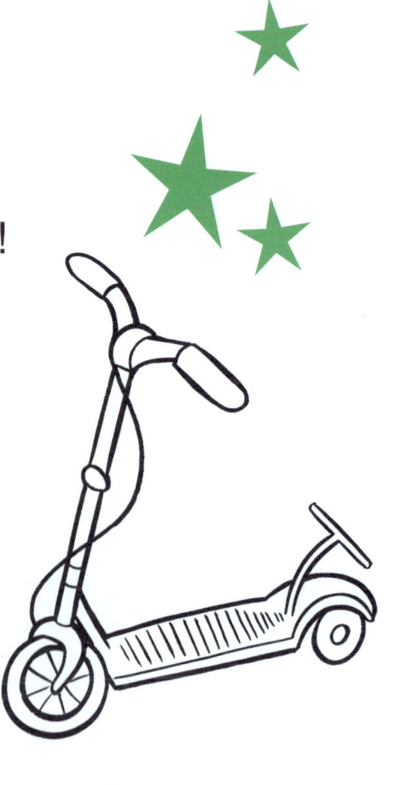

1 **Circle all the exclamation marks in the advertisement.**

2 **Write one exclamation used in the advertisement.**

3 **Tick the sentences that are exclamations.**

I can't believe it!

Do you want a drink?

Run!

4 **Underline the emotive words in the advertisement. Use the exclamations in the box to help you.**

How exciting! Sad to sell!

5 **Write your own exclamation about the green scooter.**

6 **How much is the scooter?**

7 **Write an exclamation about each picture.**

8 Rewrite the sentences with a different emotive word.

I love this basketball.

I feel happy ridding my bike.

Toy soldiers are boring.

9 What is the rule for using an exclamation mark?

10 Write your own advertisement to sell something. It could be a toy, a book or a game. Remember to use exclamations and emotive language.

Unit 18 Birds of Prey

A **simple sentence** makes sense by itself and tells us about a single idea. It starts with a **capital letter** and ends with a **full stop**. Simple sentences always have verbs. An **action verb** shows what is being done.
She jumps quickly.

Explanation

Birds of Prey

Birds of prey are strong hunters.

They skilfully catch and kill animals to eat.
There are around 300 kinds of birds of prey. They include:

- eagles
- vultures
- falcons
- kites
- hawks
- owls.

Birds of prey can see very well. The can smell and hear very well, too. They have sharp claws to swiftly catch and grip their prey. They have very sharp beaks to stab and rip their meat. All these things help them to hunt.

1 **Trace the action verbs in the explanation.**

2 **Underline one simple sentence in the explanation.**

3 **Write three adverbs from the explanation.**

______________ ______________ ______________

4 **Change the adverb to change the meaning of each sentence. The first one has been done for you.**

The girl talked loudly.

The girl talked softly.

My dog always barks.

My dog ______________ barks.

The boy ran quickly.

The boy ran ______________.

I am going to sit outside.

I am going to sit ______________.

The eagle flew high in the sky.

The eagle flew ______________ in the sky.

5 **Write an action verb for each picture.**

6 **Choose one action verb and one adverb for each picture to describe it. Write a sentence beside each picture.**

Action verbs	Adverbs
crying	loudly
driving	slowly
eating	fast
roaring	sadly

7 **Circle the action verbs. Underline the adverbs.**

hopped quietly laughed jumped loudly

8 **Write five sentences about the picture. Use action verbs and adverbs in your sentences to explain what is happening.**

Unit 19 Around Australia

Proper nouns are the names of individual people, places and things. Proper nouns always have a **capital letter**. *William went to Melbourne on Monday.*

A **past tense verb** shows what was being done in the past. *Last year I went on a trip.*

Recount

Around Australia

Last year, my family and I went on a big trip around Australia. We drove in our caravan.

We started in Melbourne and went north along the coast. We stopped in many places, including Sydney, Townsville and Cairns. We went to Cooktown near the top of Australia. Then we went west to Western Australia. We stopped in Broome, Port Headland and Perth.

Then we drove east to South Australia and stayed in Adelaide. We made it back to Melbourne after six months. Our trip was lots of fun!

1 Trace five proper nouns in the recount.

2 Write three more proper nouns from the recount.

____________ ____________ ____________

3 Draw a smiley face beside the sentence that is in the past tense.

Last year, my family went on a big trip.

Next year, my family will go to on a big trip.

4 Rewrite the proper nouns correctly.

melbourne ____________

perth ____________

adelaide ____________

5 Circle the past tense verbs.

fly	go	went	drove
walk	stopped	smile	laughed

6 Draw a picture for one of the past tense verbs in question 5.

My word: ____________

7 **Draw a line to match each present tense verb to its past tense.**

jump	ran
see	jumped
run	looked
look	saw

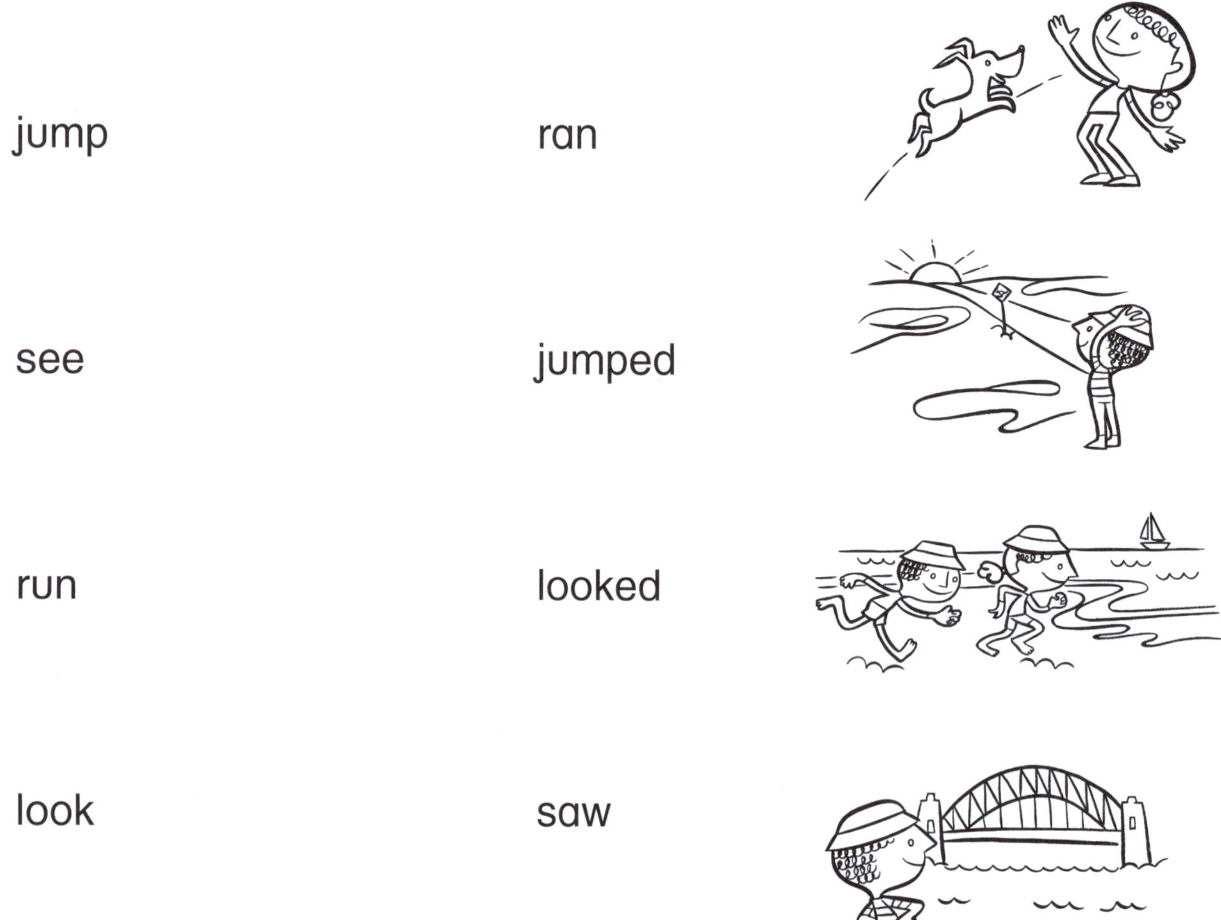

8 **Tick the sentences in the past tense.**

Three little birds hopped across the snow.

Mike took his fishing rod to the beach.

Will you play footy next week?

She likes to talk to her best friend.

I am going to catch the bus tomorrow.

He played footy yesterday.

9 **Change the underlined verbs to make them past tense.**

Tomorrow I <u>will go</u> to the shops.

Yesterday I ________________ to the shops.

Next week Jack <u>is moving</u> to Sydney.

Last week Jack ________________ to Sydney.

10 **Write a recount about a trip you have been on. Use past tense verbs. Find the place on an online map.**

____

____

____

____

____

____

____

____

Unit 20 Princess Polly

Some poems and stories have words or lines that repeat. These are called **patterns of repetition**. *Twinkle, twinkle little star.*

Some poems and stories have words that repeat the **same beginning sounds**. *Pretty Princess Polly.*

Poem

Princess Polly

Princess Polly is pretty and posh.
People who meet her say, "Oh my gosh!"
On one dark, dull and drizzly day,
Princess Polly wanted to party and play!

"I am bored in this creepy, cold castle,"
she said.

"If I don't go out now, I will go back to bed!"
So she hopped on her horse, Happy Harry Hope,
But then he went slip! Down a steep slope!

Poor Princess Polly fell off with a thud!
Poor Princess Polly fell into the mud!

1 Underline the words that start with the same sound in the poem. The first one has been done for you.

2 Fill in the gaps with words from the poem.

Poor Princess ________________

dark, dull and drizzly ________________

creepy, cold ________________

3 Draw a line to match the words with the same beginning sound.

Happy Harry	basketballs
Ben bounced	jelly
Jill juggled	slid
Sam's snake	hopped

4 Finish each sentence with a word that has the same beginning sound. The first one has been done for you.

Awesome Alex ate ___apples___.

Silly Sally saw ________________.

Lucky Lucy liked ________________.

5 **Make up a name for the cartoon characters. Each name should use the same beginning sounds.**

6 **Tick the lines in the poem that are repeated.**

Big ginger tabby cat,
I'm so glad you're not a rat.
I love cats!

Sleeping soundly on your mat,
Rolling around on your belly so fat.
I love cats!

If you could speak,
We could chat.
I love cats!

7 **Many tongue twisters use repeated sounds. Say these tongue twisters with a partner.**

Penny prefers her pretty pink piggy bank.

She sells sea shells by the sea shore.

8 **Write words that begin with the same sound as your name.**

For example: Kara: keen, koala, call, careful, kept, kite, cat.

9 **Think of a friend's name that begins with a different sound to yours. Write words that begin with that sound.**

10 **Write words that begin with the same sound as your mum's name.**

11 **Write the name of the animal that starts with the letter "s". Then write a sentence about the animal using lots of words with the "s" sound.**

Unit 21 Day and Night

A **question** is a sentence that asks something.
Why is there day and night?

A question always ends with a **question mark**.
What makes it light?

Explanation

What is day and night?

When it is light on Earth, we call it day.

When it is dark on Earth, we call it night.

Why is it light?

It is light because the Sun is shining on Earth.

Why is it dark?

The Sun only shines on one side of Earth at a time.

The side that the Sun does not shine on is dark.

Why does it change from light to dark?

The Earth is always turning.

So, the side facing the Sun during the day will face away from the Sun at night.

1 **Trace the lines under the questions in the explanation.**

2 **Circle all the question marks in the explanation.**

3 **Practise writing question marks.**

4 **Add a question mark or a full stop to each sentence.**

What is day and night ☐

When the Sun shines on Earth it is light ☐

The Earth is always turning ☐

Why does it change from light to dark ☐

5 **Draw a line to match the question to its answer.**

Is the Earth round?	A pilot flies an aeroplane.
When do leaves fall off trees?	Yes, the Earth is round.
Who flies an aeroplane?	Leaves fall off trees in autumn.

6 **Read the list. Write three words that can start a question.**

why shirt when who dog cat gate

______ ______ ______

7 **Look at the picture. Write some questions about the picture. Remember to use a question mark at the end.**

What ______

When ______

Where ______

Who ______

Why ______

8 **Colour the sun yellow and the rocket red in the picture above.**

9 Write an explanation all about you. Write questions and answers about yourself.

All About Me!

10 Draw a picture of yourself playing at your favourite place.

Unit 22 What a Party!

A **personal pronoun** takes the place of a noun.
Josh went down the slide. He went down the slide.

Formal language is used when a person's spoken language is not suitable, such as in a letter.

Thank-You Letter

68 Bell Street
Merryville
Thursday 20 October

Dear Luke,

Thank you for inviting me to your Superhero birthday party.

Fun Land was great. They have so many things to do. My favourite thing was the long red slide. I went down it so fast. It was funny when Josh went down the slide backwards. His cape went over his head!

I want to have my party at Fun Land, too. I asked Mum. She said she will think about it.

See you at footy!

From

Patrick

1 **Underline all the personal pronouns in the letter.**

2 **Write four personal pronouns from the letter.**

________________ ________________

________________ ________________

3 **Circle the date.**

4 **Shade the formal words in the letter. Use the words in the box to help you.**

Dear Luke
Thank you for inviting me
From Patrick

5 **Draw a smiley face beside the sentences that use formal language.**

Hey Kate, let's go outside.

Hello, Mrs Anderson.

Where's my jumper?

Wow! That ride was so cool!

May I please put the flag on the sandcastle?

Wait for me!

6 Fill in the gaps with a pronoun.

my you She I me you

Dear Abby,

How are ____________?

I am writing to ask if you would like to come to ____________

house on Friday. Mum can pick ____________ up after school.

____________ will buy us pizza for dinner.

Please let ____________ know tomorrow if you can make it.

____________ hope you can!

From

Ella

7 Finish the sentences with words from the list.

Patrick you the Land He

Thank ____________ for inviting me.

See you at ____________ footy.

Fun ____________ was great!

From ____________

____________ went down the slide.

8 **Write a letter to an uncle or aunt you don't know very well. Remember to use personal pronouns and formal language.**

Address: ______________________

____

Date: ______________________

To: ______________

____

____

____

____

____

____

From

____

Unit 23 Treasure Map

A **preposition** gives extra information about the noun in a sentence. *He walks over the bridge.*

A sentence that tells us what to do is a **command**. *Walk over the bridge.* Commands can have prepositions in them.

Directions

Treasure Map

Look at the map and follow the commands to find the treasure.

1 Get out of the boat.

2 Walk over the sand.

3 Go past the palm trees.

4 Walk across the bridge.

5 Crawl through the cave.

6 Walk through the forest.

7 Find the big rock.

8 Dig! Dig! Dig!

1 **On the map, draw the path you take to find the treasure. Put a big X where you need to dig.**

2 **Trace the underline below three prepositions in the treasure map. Underline three other prepositions.**

3 **Write three prepositions from the treasure map directions.**

____________ ____________ ____________

4 **Draw a picture to match each command.**

Get out of the boat.

Walk across the bridge.

5 **Draw a line to match the picture to a sentence. Underline the prepositions.**

The girl crawled through the cave.

The boy walked between the palm trees.

The dog buried the bone in a hole.

The man walked along the tightrope.

6 **Fill the gaps with a preposition.**

on outside in near under

The fish is ________________ the fish tank.

The cat is ________________ the table.

The fish tank is ________________ the table.

The dog is ________________ the room.

Some mice are ________________ the cat.

7 **Write a command for each picture.**

____

____

____

____

8 Write the prepositions you have learned today.

9 Make your own treasure map! Draw your treasure map and write some commands so people can find the treasure.

Find the treasure!

Unit 24 Super Gran!

An **action verb** is a word that shows what is being done – a "doing" word. *Super Gran ran fast.*

Informal language is used to show a person's everyday spoken language. *Ha ha! Funny!*

Comic Strip

Super Gran!

1 **Circle all the action verbs in the comic. Use the words in the box to help you.**

Jump! Fly! Grab! Land!

2 **Underline the action verbs below.**

run table throw cape ticket slide flower ski

3 **Write an action verb for each picture.**

pedal jump kick speed spin twirl leap race

_______________ _______________

_______________ _______________

4 **Tick the sentences that use informal language.**

Excuse me, how may I help you?

Can I help you?

My dear friend, would you like to visit me at my home?

Hey, want to chill at my place?

We'll be there in five.

We will arrive in five minutes.

5 **Fill the gaps with an action verb.**

Ethan ____________________ as fast as he could to win the race.

The eagle ____________________ high in the sky.

Sienna ____________________ the tree to get her frisbee.

6 **Write each word in a comic strip style. Here are some examples:**

fast FAST

jump JUMP

tiny

bang

tall

 7 **Make your own comic! You will need to draw pictures and write captions and speech bubbles. Remember to use action verbs.**

8 **Write a sentence using these informal words.**

Wow! ____________________

Ha ha! ____________________

Hurry up! ____________________

Unit 25 Super Gran Again!

An **adjective** is a word that describes a noun.
Sweet, *old*, *cheeky* and *little* are all adjectives.

A **present tense verb** shows what is happening now.
I can see Gran.

Narrative

Super Gran Again!

My neighbour is a sweet, gentle old lady. We call her Gran. I can see Gran outside in her front yard. My cheeky little sister is outside too. She is playing with her big, bouncy ball.

Suddenly, I see my sister's ball rolling onto the busy road. She runs after it.

"Stop!" I yell, but she doesn't hear me.
I start to run.

Gran runs and grabs my sister and the ball, all in a split second!

"Wow," I think. "Gran is not what she seems!"

1 **Trace over the adjectives in the narrative.**

2 **Underline three present tense verbs in the narrative.**

3 **Write three adjectives that are used to describe Gran.**
The first one has been done for you.

sweet ____________ ____________ ____________

4 **Draw a line to match each present tense word with a picture.**

bounce

roll

run

5 **Circle the sentence in each pair that is in the present tense.**

I walk fast.

I walked fast.

I had a cold.

I have a cold.

I bounce the ball.

I bounced the ball.

6 **Write each word in the present tense.**

played ______________

cooked ______________

painted ______________

7 **Write three more verbs in the present tense.**

______________ ______________ ______________

8 **Write a sentence that describes what Kitty looks like in the picture. Use adjectives in your sentence.**

____

____

9 **Write a sentence about what Kitty is doing. Use present tense verbs.**

____

____

10 **Fill in the gaps with the correct adjective from the box.**

pretty cold fast

The __________ wind blows.

The __________ car went down the road.

The girl picked some __________ flowers.

11 **Write your own narrative about Super Gran. Write in the present tense. Use adjectives to make your story interesting.**

Super Gran!

Glossary

action verb	an action word that shows what someone or something is doing
adjective	a word that describes a noun
adverb	a word that tells you more about a verb
capital letter	a letter used at the start of a sentence and the start of a proper noun
command	a sentence that tells someone to do something
common noun	a word that names a general group of people, places, animals and things
compound word	a word made from two smaller words
descriptive sentence	a sentence that uses many adjectives and adverbs
direct speech	actual words spoken by the speaker
emotive language	words that try to make you feel something
exclamation	a sentence that shows strong emotion
exclamation mark	a mark (!) used after an exclamation
formal language	language used for certain occasions and ceremonies; not everyday language
full stop	a mark (.) used at the end of a sentence
indirect speech	tells about what was said; not the actual spoken words
informal language	everyday language; used in spoken language
noun	a word that names people, places, animals and things
number adjective	a word that shows how many of something there is
past tense verb	a word that shows what was being done in the past
personal pronoun	a word that takes the place of a noun
precise language	language that uses words that are clear and to the point
preposition	a word that shows the position of a noun
present tense verb	a word that shows what is being done now

proper noun	the actual name of a person, a place or a thing
question	a sentence that asks something
question mark	a mark (?) at the end of a question
quotation marks	marks (“ ”) that are placed around what is being said
simple sentence	a group of words about a single idea
statement	a sentence that gives true information about something
verb	a word that shows what someone or something is doing

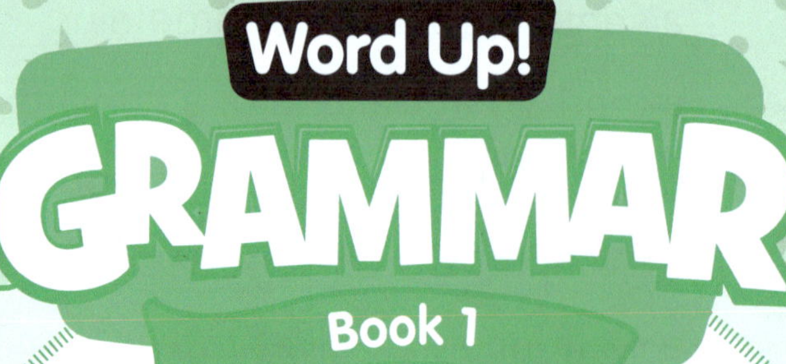

This is to certify that

....

is a Grammar Guru

Signed ....

School ....

Date ....

GRAMMAR GURU